Telugu Padaalu *with* Bommalu

A Portal To Learn Telugu

Author : Bhaavya Ram

This book is dedicated to all my Gurus (My Elementary School Teachers, Maddipaadu, Prakasam District, Andhra Pradesh, India)
who taught me how to read and write the wonderful language that is, Telugu.

Table of Contents

అక్షరాలు (Alphabets) — 3
అచ్చులు (Vowels) — 6
హల్లులు (consonants) — 7
బొమ్మలు (pictures) — 10
Disclaimer — 57
Acknowledgement — 58

అక్షరాలు (Alphabets)

How many alphabets we have?

52

How do you classify them?

52 alphabets are classified into
1. Vowels
2. Consonants

Vowels

అ ఆ ఇ ఈ ఉ ఊ
ఋ ౠ ఎ ఏ ఐ
ఒ ఓ ఔ
అం అః

****

Consonants

క ఖ గ ఘ జ
చ ఛ జ ఝ ఞ
ట ఠ డ ఢ ణ
త థ ద ధ న
ప ఫ బ భ మ
య ర ల వ శ
ష స హ ళ క్ష ఱ

****

అచ్చులు (Vowels)

అ	a
ఆ	Long a
ఇ	i
ఈ	ee
ఉ	u
ఊ	Long u
ఋ	ru
ౠ	roo
ఎ	e
ఏ	Long e
ఐ	i/y
ఒ	o
ఓ	Long o
ఔ	ow
అం	am
అః	aha

హల్లులు (consonants)

క	ka
ఖ	kha
గ	ga
ఘ	gha
ఙ	inya
చ	cha
ఛ	chha
జ	ja
ఝ	jha
ఞ	ini
ట	ta
ఠ	tta
డ	da
ఢ	dda

ణ	nna
త	tha
థ	thha
ద	dha
ధ	dhha
న	na
ప	pa
ఫ	pha
బ	ba
భ	bha
మ	ma
య	ya
ర	ra
ల	la
వ	va
శ	ssa

ష	sha
స	sa
హ	ha
ళ	lla
క్ష	ksha
ఱ	rra

****

బొమ్మలు(pictures)

అ as

అమ్మ(a mma)

1.Mother

****

ఆ as

ఆవు(aa vu)

2.Cow

****

ఇ as

ఇల్లు (I llu)

3. House

****

ఈ as

ఈగ (ee ga)

4. Housefly

****

ఊ as
ఉడుత(u du tha)

5.Squirrel

****

ఊ as
ఊయల (oo ya la)

6.Swing

****

ఋ as

ఋతువులు (ru thu vu lu)

7. Seasons

****

ఎ as
ఎలుక (e lu ka)

8.Rat

****

ఏ as
ఏనుగు(ae nu gu)

9.Elephant

****

ఐ as

ఐదు (I du)

10.Five

****

ಒ as

ಒಂಟೆ (o nte)

11. Camel

****

ఓ as
ఓడ (ao da)

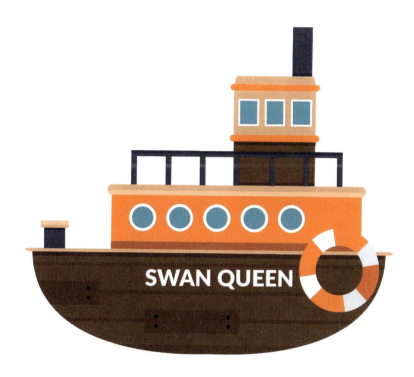

12.Ship

****

ఔ as
ఔషధము(ow sha da mu)

13.Medicine

****

ఆం as

అంకెలు(am ke lu)

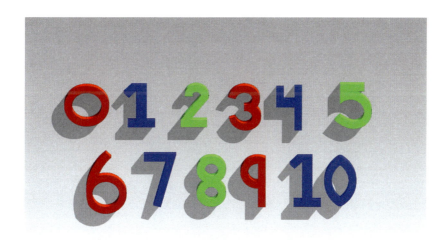

14.Numbers

****

క as కయాక్ (ka yaa k)

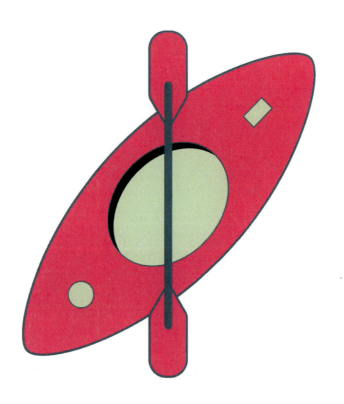

15.Kayak

****

ఖ as

ఖర్జురము (Kha rju ra mu)

16.Dates

****

గ as
గడ్డి (ga ddi)

17.Grass

****

ఘ as ఘటము(gha ta mu)

18.Pot

****

చ as
చదువు(cha du vu)

19.Reading

****

ఛ as ఛత్రము (chha tra mu)

20. Umbrella

****

ජ as

ජඩ(ja da)

21.Braid

****

ట as
టపాసులు(ta paa su lu)

22.Firecrackers

****

ర as
కంఠము(kam tta mu)

23.Neck

****

డ as
డబ్బు(da bbu)

24.Money

****

ఢ as
ఢంకా (ddam kaa)

25. drum

****

ణ as
బాణము(baa nna mu)

26.Arrow

****

త as

తల

27.Head

****

థ as
పథము(pa thha mu)

28.Road

****

ద as
దండ(dham da)

29.Garland

****

ధ as

ధార(dhhaa ra)

30.Flow

న as
నక్క (na kka)

31. Fox

****

ప as
పండు(pam du)

32.Fruit

****

ఫ as ఫలము(pha la mu)

33.Seethaphalamu

****

బ as
బండి(bam di)

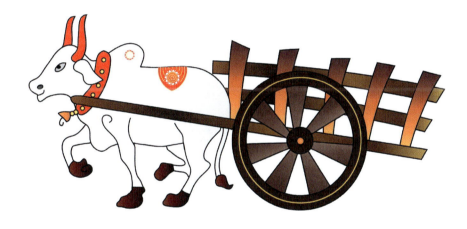

34.Vehicle

****

భ as

భౌ(bhow)

35.Bhow bhow

****

మ as
మంచు(mam chu)

36.Snow

****

య as
యజ్ఞము(ya jna mu)

37.Homam

****

ర as
రంగవల్లి (ram ga va lli)

38.Rangavall

ල as
ලතා (la tha)

39.Creeper

****

వ as
వడియాలు(va di yaa lu)

40.vadiyalu

****

శ as
శనగలు(ssa na ga lu)

41.Chickpeas

****

ష as

బాదూష(baa dhoo sha)

42.Badusha

****

స as
సరస్సు(sa ra ssu)

43.Lake

****

హా as
హంస(ham sa)

44.Swan

****

ళ as కళలు(ka lla lu)

45.Arts

****

క్ష as
క్షీరం(kshee ram)

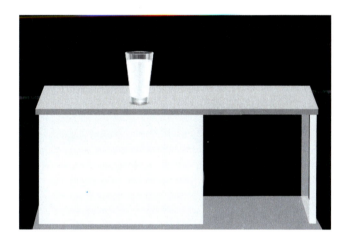

46.Milk

****

ఆ as
గుర్రము(gu rrra mu)

47.Horse

****

Disclaimer

While all attempts have been made to verify the information provided in this Book, neither the Author nor the Publisher assumes any responsibility for errors, omissions, or contrary interpretations of the subject matter herein.

This Book is for educational purposes only. Any results obtained by readers following the instructions in this Book will vary based on skill level and individual perception of the contents herein, and thus no guarantees, monetarily or otherwise, can be made accurately. Therefore, no guarantees of any kind are made.

The views expressed are those of the Author alone, and should not be taken as expert instruction or commands. The reader is responsible for his/her own actions. Neither the Author nor the Publisher assumes any responsibility or liability whatsoever on behalf of the purchase or reader of this Book.

Acknowledgement

Writing this book was totally inspired by my 3 children, who wanted to learn Telugu.
The writing of this book was supported
By our family and friends.

Most of the Images are customized

Images 2,3,4,5,6,7,9,11,12,13,15,16,17,18,19,32,45 and 46
by
www.fiverr.com/ajay13890

Images 10,14
by
www.fiverr.com/legal_drawingz

Images 8,20,21,22,23,25,27,28,31,34,35,37,43,44 and 47
by
www.fiverr.com/rizvi_memon

Images 1,24,26 and 29
by
www.fiverr.com/kingsukemma

Images 30,36
Skitch App

Image 33
by
Hudhayambika Burramukku

Image 38
by
Sowmya Gowda

and

Images 39, 40, 41 and 42
by
Ramyambika Burramukku

****

Made in the USA
Middletown, DE
15 August 2020